HIDDEN MUSIC

Hidden Music

THE LIFE OF FANNY MENDELSSOHN

by

Gloria Kamen

ATHENEUM BOOKS FOR YOUNG READERS

Atheneum Books for Young Readers
An imprint of Simon & Schuster Children's Publishing Division
1230 Avenue of the Americas
New York, New York 10020

Designed by Laura Hammond Hough
The text of this book is set in Centaur.
The illustrations are rendered in ink and watercolors.

FIRST EDITION

Printed in the United States of America

10 9 8 7 6 5 4 3 2 1

Library of Congress Cataloging-in-Publication Data
Kamen, Gloria
    Hidden music : the life of Fanny Mendelssohn / by Gloria Kamen.
        p.   cm.
    Includes bibliographical references and index.
    Summary : Describes the life of Felix Mendelssohn's sister, a highly talented
composer in her own right.
    ISBN 0-689-31714-X
    1. Hensel, Fanny Mendelssohn, 1805–1847. 2. Women composers—Germany—
Biography—Juvenile literature. [1. Hensel, Fanny Mendelssohn, 1805–1847. 2.
Composers. 3. Women—Biography.]
I. Title.
ML3930.H46K36   1996
786.2'092—dc20
[B]   95-15215

*To the memory of Norma Hexter,
friend,
compassionate teacher,
and lover of music.*

Contents

Acknowledgments

$\mathcal{M}$any people have generously helped in my search for details of the life of this modest but talented woman. My special thanks go first to Professor Marcia J. Citron of the Shepard School of Music, Rice University, whose edition of Fanny's letters to Felix was an enormous source of information, as well as for her help in going over my book before its publication. My thanks to her publisher, Pendragon Press, for permission to use numerous excerpts of her translation of Fanny's letters from the book, *The Letters of Fanny Hensel to Felix Mendelssohn* (1987).

To Dr. James W. Pruett, Chief of the Music Division of the Library of Congress, for his help in locating new sources of information and for his suggestions, my thanks. To Lydia Artymiw, a fine concert pianist and teacher, my thanks for reviewing an early version of this book. To Professor David Grayson of the University of Minnesota, who so carefully corrected my errors in that same version as well as offering his excellent comments, I owe special thanks.

My thanks also go to Dr. Hans-Gunter Klein, Director

of the Staatsbibliothek Zu Berlin, Preussischer Kulturbesitz, where much of the Mendelssohn archives exist, for his information regarding Fanny Hensel's letters and music.

Without the help of my friends, Gene Namovicz, Peggy Thomson, Marguerite Murray, and Charlotte Berman, all of whom gave me the kind of constructive criticism needed to pull the book together, my job would have seemed endless. As always thanks are in order to my editor, Marcia Marshall, and to my husband, Elliot, both of whom are always an enormous help when I am writing a book.

To Bard College for arranging a Mendelssohn festival, which included Fanny's music, and to Professor R. Larry Todd for his book on the family, my thanks. And, finally, to the musicians and publishers of newly recorded compact discs of Fanny Hensel's music I offer my applause.

HIDDEN MUSIC

*Lea and
Abraham Mendelssohn*

∽ *Chapter 1* ∽

The Gift

The extraordinary talent of your children wants direction, not forcing.

Abraham Mendelssohn, January 1818

*E*ver since she was a little girl Fanny found it hard to disguise her feelings. Her face gave her away; the turn of her mouth, the line between her dark eyebrows showed when she was displeased. Even more revealing were her eyes, eyes that mirrored her feelings when she tried hard to hide them. Her younger brother Felix could always guess before she said a word whether she enjoyed the music he had just played for her.

Now, as she sat at the pianoforte in the large music room of their house in Berlin, hands in her lap, her eyes closed for a brief moment, all was quiet. This would be a gift to her father, a surprise concert for his birthday. She was about to play the music written by her mother's favorite composer, Johann Sebastian Bach. In preparation for this day she had spent months practicing Bach's Well-Tempered Clavier in order to play it entirely from memory.

Fanny knew her father loved music though he never learned to play an instrument himself. Her mother, Lea, however, was an accomplished pianist whose teacher had studied with Bach. The music was so familiar to her, she

I

would surely catch any wrong notes because she often played Bach's music herself. But Fanny was certain it would be her younger brother Felix who would listen with the greatest attention and admiration.

Now that even little sister Rebecka was quietly settled in her seat, Fanny was ready to begin. Carefully positioning her hands above the keys, with a look of deep concentration on her face, she began to play. Her music would be a gift for her mother, too. When Fanny was born, thirteen years ago, her mother, touching her tiny baby's beautifully formed fingers, told her husband that their little daughter had "Bach fugue fingers." Someday, she was sure, those same hands would be able to play the famous composer's difficult piano music. Her prediction was about to be proven correct.

For the next two hours Fanny's hands moved easily and flawlessly over the keyboard as her family listened in hushed amazement. When she finished, Fanny looked around and smiled shyly. Was her mother impressed? And her father, was he pleased? Her mother, Fanny could tell, was openly proud. Her father said not a word, he seemed stunned. But it was Felix who was the first to jump up to congratulate her. He had expected her to succeed, and she had.

The concert was a fitting gift for her father, for he had spared no expense in finding his children the best music teachers in the city of Berlin. Talent, he believed, must go hand in hand with first-rate training, though he himself was not offered this luxury as a child. But in Lea Salomon's family playing piano was a tradition that would naturally be passed on from mother to daughter.

Abraham Mendelssohn's words of praise did not come until a few days later in a letter he wrote to his wife while on a business trip. It always seemed easier for him to express his feelings in writing than face-to-face. While offering lavish praise to Fanny for "the wonderful achievement of learning twenty-four preludes by heart," and to Lea for "your perseverence in superintending her practicing," he added:

> [Her concert] made me speechless with astonishment, and I have only [now] recovered the use of my voice to make this great success known. But with you and Fanny I must confess that I think the thing decidedly *blamable*: the exertion is too great, and might easily have hurt her. The extraordinary talent of your children wants direction, not forcing.

Forcing? Fanny's father could not have been more mistaken, for it was not Lea who pushed Fanny into giving a two-hour-long concert. Her performance had nothing to do with *forcing* and everything to do with Fanny's love of Bach's music and love of a challenge. By age thirteen young Fanny had already surpassed her mother's musical talent and was eager to go beyond her parents' modest aim of making her a cultured and talented young woman whose ability to play music would help find her a good husband.

Both Fanny and nine and a half-year-old Felix were seriously attached to music in a way their father found hard to understand.

Karl
Friedrich
Zelter

Chapter 2

The Education of Fanny and Felix

I will tell you today, dear Fanny, that in all essential points, all that is important, I am so much satisfied with you that I have no wish left.

Abraham Mendelssohn, November 1828

Though Fanny was sure her father was pleased with her concert for his birthday, the pleasure had been mixed with some anxiety. Fanny's music lessons, begun in an informal way with her mother, were later joined by her brother when he turned five. In four years Felix had all but caught up with Fanny and a certain friendly competition had begun. She wondered if it was wrong to compete, if her display of talent had been misunderstood.

Each day, Fanny and Felix shared the nursery and music room from early morning till night, working at lessons and playing together more like twins than elder sister and younger brother. As children of a successful banker they were expected to undergo the kind of challenging training that their mother had had as a child. Lea Salomon was the granddaughter of the wealthy Daniel Isaac Itzig, probably one of the richest men in all of Prussia in the late 1790s. Lea was reared with all the privileges of the very wealthy, but at the same time she was required to learn the skills considered necessary for any cultured woman of her day. She was taught to speak several languages, a bit of math and literature, and how to play music. What had been left out and what she had little knowledge of, however, was life outside her sheltered surroundings.

Lea's children were taught by hired tutors at home, a home run by their strict authoritarian father. The day began at five in the morning for Fanny and Felix with instructions in math, literature, drawing, and of course, music. Some time was set aside for physical exercise and dance lessons for Fanny and her younger sister. While Fanny was a concientious student and worked at all her lessons, it was clear from the start that her main interest was music. It seemed only natural that this should be so for Lea not only gave her her first piano lessons but also named her Fanny Cecilia after two of her mother's great-aunts: Fanny von Arnstein and Cecilia von Eskeles. Both aunts, inheritors of great wealth and owners of elegant estates, arranged private concerts for and were supporters of some of the greatest Austrian and German composers of their day. The great Ludwig van Beethoven had often performed in Baroness von Arnstein's home only fifteen years before Fanny was born. These concerts were famous throughout Austria, Germany, and northern Italy. Baroness von Eskeles also had many well-known musicians perform at her lavish estate. Lea particularly admired these two aunts and kept close contact with them for most of her life.

Among the women who studied music in the Itzig family there were several talented musicians, but none of them ever considered becoming professional performers for this would have gone against the unwritten rules of their society. Women, it was understood at the time, only earned money as a necessity, never just to display a talent. That could be done as a talented "dilettante," a French word meaning anyone who did things for the love of it, not for money. For members of the upper class, especially women, to perform for hire would be considered immodest and somewhat disgraceful.

Neither was it acceptable to be seen as idle or lazy. Every hour of Fanny's day, as it had been for her mother, was carefully structured by her parents who equated free time with idleness. Music, therefore, became Fanny's and Felix's outlet for dreaming, for expressing emotion, and for being creative. Even after their younger sister Rebecka and little brother Paul shared the playroom and lessons, Fanny and Felix maintained their special closeness. They had little contact, in fact, with other children their age, except for those belonging to relatives and close friends. Even on vacations, taken in a caravan of horse-driven coaches filled with family members and a few friends, they weren't free to roam on their own. It was the custom in the early 1800s (Fanny was born in 1805) for girls of Fanny's social class to be constantly under the watchful eye of an adult. It's no wonder then that without other close friendships Fanny became so dependent on her brother for companionship and support.

Felix was a particularly handsome child with soft brown hair that curled down to his shoulders, framing a finely chiseled profile. As a young girl, Fanny most resembled her mother, a lively-looking, but not an especially pretty woman, whose most striking features were her dark expressive eyes and finely shaped hands. Fanny's small frame, though slightly marred by one shoulder being higher than the other, was elegant and shapely. Like their parents, both children had quick, agile minds, making each a perfect foil for the other, and they accepted and seemed to thrive on strict discipline.

From the time she was little, Fanny was well behaved, eager to please her parents, especially her father, for as caring as Abraham was for his children, he was not given to either praising them or to displays of affection. He expected and received full obedience to his rules. Rules were what he had lived by in order to succeed. His childhood, in direct contrast to his wife's, had been anything but comfortable and privileged. His father had started life poor and unknown. By making the right choices at the right time, Abraham had overcome his lack of formal education and status to achieve remarkable success in the business world.

Fanny's grandfather, Moses Mendelssohn, had come to the Prussian city of Berlin from Dessau in 1743 at age fourteen with little more than the clothes on his back and an intense desire to better himself. He settled in the Berlin ghetto, a section of the city set aside for Jews, who were forbidden at that time from owning property or renting in other areas of the city. He attended a ghetto school set up for Jewish children when Prussian schools were closed to them. Because of the restrictions, many Jews in the ghettos never learned to read and write in German. Children like Moses studied in Hebrew, not German. But Moses had a talent for languages and taught himself French, German, Latin, and Greek. His keen intellect and natural charm later earned him not only the respect of the Jewish community but made him friendships outside the ghetto as well.

Despite a hunched back, Moses had no trouble finding a wife who later bore him six children. Fanny's father was their second son. While earning a modest living as a bookkeeper and then as a silk merchant, in his spare time Moses wrote books on philosophy and religion, his most ambitious being a translation of the first five books of the Old Testament from Hebrew into German. By placing the languages side by side Moses hoped to help his fellow Jews learn the language of the country in which they were living. Through his books Moses' reputation as a defender of Judaism spread throughout Europe.

Fanny's knowledge about her grandfather came mostly from his books, for Moses died when her father was only ten years old. His death brought an end to Abraham's formal education. From then on he was taught by his older brother and sisters, who also helped support him.

When he was twenty-one, Abraham moved to Paris, where he spent several years working for a banking house, then returned to Hamburg to form his own banking and import firm with an older brother. In Hamburg Abraham married Lea Salomon and the following year they had their first child.

The Mendelssohn banking firm prospered, but in 1811, war was spreading throughout Europe. Fanny had just turned six, Felix was two and a half, and sister Rebecka was only a few months old. Moving eastward from France, Napoleon's army invaded Hamburg. It was the beginning of widespread looting in the city and a hunt for those who had actively supported the Prussian side. Abraham was one of those supporters. The Mendelssohns fled to Berlin and then to Paris where Fanny's Aunt Henriette was living. In Paris, eleven-year-old Fanny had her first professional music lessons with Marie Bigot, a popular French pianist, and her first taste of living in another country. After a year, they returned to Berlin where their everyday routine of study and music lessons continued as before.

For Fanny's father the changes that followed worked in his favor. The victorious French passed laws allowing more freedom to those not protected by the old Prussian laws. Some of the Jews and the poorest segment of society, serfs and peasants, were given new rights. During this wave of political tolerance, Prince Hardenberg, then chancellor of Prussia (Berlin was its capital), gave legal equality to many German Jews. Serfdom, a form of economic slavery, was abolished.

But just ten years later, when Prince Hardenberg died, his reforms were reversed. The constant change of rules created terrible anxiety among the Jews who, like the Mendelssohns, had begun to take their new status for granted.

Abraham saw only two alternatives to putting up once again with second-class citizenship: one was to leave Prussia for a country where the laws were more tolerant, as many did; the other, to change their identity and religion. Unlike his father who willingly fought for what he believed, Abraham chose what he considered the safer, easier route. To abandon his country and a successful banking business was to him unthinkable. Taking Moses Mendelssohn's effort to integrate Jews into German society beyond his intention, some members of the Salomon and Mendelssohn families had converted to either the Catholic or Lutheran faith some years earlier. Lea's brother took the further step of adopting a different last name. Instead of Jacob *Salomon*, a recognizably Jewish name, he called himself Jacob *Bartholdy*.

In 1816, all the Mendelssohn children were baptized as Christians. Before this, religious practices seemed to have been minimal in their family, and apparently continued so after their conversion. Fanny, the ever obedient daughter, would hardly have questioned her parents' decision, and there seems to have been little discussion about the conversion within the family.

Once again her father found it easier to express his strongest feelings in a letter instead of face-to-face. He tried to explain to Fanny at the time of her confirmation why abandoning her religion was logical and right in his eyes. As her father, he said, he wanted to protect his children from the anti-Semitism he had known. If there was to be renewed anti-Semitism, it would be safer and more sensible not to have to deal with it, he said. He hoped that in the future his children would live in a world where they could safely and honestly practice any religion they chose.

Changing religions was not easy for Abraham. The name Mendelssohn was too strongly linked with the Jewish philosophy of his renowned father to abandon it lightly. But Abraham was fearful that his sons might someday be handicapped with a recognizably Jewish name, and agonized over whether to change it.

In letters between Lea's brother Jacob Bartholdy and Abraham the question was hotly argued. After dismissing Abraham's arguments for loyalty to his father's name, Jacob suggested as an alternative the use of a hyphenated name: that of Mendelssohn-Bartholdy. This was the solution Abraham ultimately adopted and later had to justify to his grown children. Below the surface of their elegant and privileged life was a need to conform to the rules of a sometimes hostile and unpredictable society. This mixture of success and anxiety about the future surely helped reenforce Abraham's rigid view of how Fanny should spend her life.

Despite all the political unrest, Abraham was able to maintain a successful business. In 1817, the family moved from their modest house in Berlin to a large mansion in a parklike setting on Leipziger Strasse. The house, with its large conservatory opening onto seven acres of garden and woodlands, was in a state of neglect. Some of the walls and ceilings were covered with elegant but damaged fresco paintings. After considerable renovation, the house once again became one of the most elegant homes in the city of Berlin. The conservatory, capable of accommodating a large audience, became a place to hold private concerts, continuing the von Arnstein and Salomon tradition. While only invited guests were welcomed to these regular Sunday concerts, this sometimes included as many as one hundred fifty people.

These guests were generally a critical and musically educated group of friends and relatives who expected classical music of the highest quality.

Around the age of thirteen or fourteen, after proving her skill as a pianist, Fanny and then Felix, when he was old enough, joined in the Sunday performances with the whole-hearted encouragement of their parents.

At times, little Felix, standing on a box, was allowed to conduct a group of musicians while Fanny, dressed in her prettiest dress, watched. It would be another twenty years before Fanny would be allowed to conduct an orchestra.

Chapter 3

Separate Ways

*Music will perhaps become his profession, whilst for you it can and
must only be an ornament, never the root of your being and doing.*
Abraham Mendelssohn, July 1820

The first long separation of brother and sister occurred
when Felix was twelve. It was the first sign of the way music,
which had tied them together, would also pull them apart.

It began with an invitation from Karl Zelter, who taught
them music theory, asking Felix to accompany him on an
extended vacation trip. They would be going to Weimar to
see Zelter's friend, the famous poet-philosopher Johann
Wolfgang von Goethe. Zelter wanted to show off Felix's talent, knowing the great German writer would enjoy hearing
the boy play the music of some of Goethe's favorite composers. To perform for Goethe was a great honor, especially
for someone as young as Felix. Before he left, Fanny insisted
that he send her the smallest details of his trip so that she
could share just a little of this historic visit. She couldn't
admit to any jealousy, even to herself.

Excited and somewhat awed by the attention he received
Felix wrote to Fanny, "Every morning I receive a kiss from
the author of *Faust* and of *Werther* . . . Fancy that!! In the
afternoon I played [piano] for two hours, in part fugues by
Bach, in part I improvised."

Felix Mendelssohn,
age sixteen

Luigi
Cherubini

Continuing his description of the visit he wrote:

> In the evening we all ate together, even Goethe, who
> usually never eats at night. Now my dear coughing
> Fanny [Fanny's cough was always a sign that she disap-
> proved of something when she was reluctant to say so
> in words], early yesterday I showed your songs to Frau
> von Goethe, who has a pretty voice. She is going to
> sing them for the old gentleman [Goethe]. I also told
> him already that you wrote them . . . Frau von Goethe
> is especially fond of them. A good omen.

Fanny's songs, called "lieder" in German, were based on
poetry, some by Goethe. Fanny was pleased to hear this
modest praise of her original music, but it was Felix who
had made such an impression as a budding talent. Seventy-
three-year-old Goethe told his friend Zelter he'd welcome
other visits from this talented boy—but made no mention
of welcoming his talented sister as well.

Felix's letters became the major event in Fanny's very quiet,
routine life. As his sister requested, he sent letters filled with
lively descriptions of what he had seen, whom he had met,
the music he heard or played. When letters didn't arrive
Fanny would lament that if it continued, her life would be
extremely boring. For fifteen-year-old Fanny, Felix was her
window to the outside world.

On a visit to a small village near Kemberg, Germany,
Felix told her about seeing a "Euphon," a relative of the
glass harmonica. The "Euphon," he explained, was made of
glass rods that are moistened and then stroked with wet fingers, the sound resulting in something like glass chimes. "So
you can easily imagine, dear Fanny, what this instrument
sounds like. We then retired to our feather beds and slept

poorly. Professor Zelter complained his bed was too short and his daughter complained about the bugs in hers."

Before daybreak, Felix wrote, he felt someone pull back the covers. It was the professor. Asked what he wanted, Herr Zelter answered, "I dreamed that someone had stolen you from me and I wanted to see if you were still there!!!"

Clearly Karl Zelter was fond of Felix and an active supporter of his early talent, and Fanny felt the difference. In a later letter, Fanny wrote, "Tell the Herr Professor [meaning their teacher, Zelter] that I find him very disloyal. He writes only to his fair-haired boy and doesn't send even one greeting to his earnest, best female student. But," she added politely, "send him my warmest regards."

A lifelong correspondence between brother and sister started when Felix began his travels. From Fanny's first letters to Felix her dependence on him for support and affection is very clear. He was the only one who seemed to understand her need for music, her urge to be creative. In other words, it was he who took her seriously as an artist.

Though older by only three and a half years Fanny sometimes playfully called Felix her *dear son*, and he, in turn called her *my dear Fenchel* or *dear Fance*, nicknames used only within the family. Despite saying in her reply to him, "Don't forget that you're my right hand and my eyesight, and without you, therefore, I can't proceed with music," Fanny kept up her usual practice at the pianoforte, though certainly with less pleasure. By then playing music together had grown into *composing* music together, songs, piano pieces, and even attempts at more ambitious works.

"You're really missed, dear son," wrote Fanny while Felix accompanied his father on a business trip to Frankfurt. "Music in particular doesn't come easy without you . . . Think of me when I turn sixteen."

Fanny's music matured between the ages of fifteen and

seventeen. She composed many piano pieces and songs, including the ones sung for the Goethes. Felix had already attempted writing two operettas and a symphony by the time he reached fifteen. His less ambitious compositions were performed for friends at home and when he traveled to other cities with his father or teacher. But the eleven sonatas Fanny wrote during those early years are either lost or in private collections since they've never been published. Who besides her family heard this music is not known. They may have been played at the semiprofessional Singakademie, directed by Zelter, where Fanny was a member of the choir and often performed on the piano. Or they may have been performed and first heard at a Mendelssohn Sunday concert. Except for Felix who surely knew their merit and listened to them critically, they were never reviewed or noted.

By the time Felix was sixteen, a well-traveled and self-assured young man, and Fanny just past nineteen, they were exploring new and more original musical forms in their compositions. It was then they created the music for a play that they had staged as children in the garden of their home in Berlin. The play, translated from English to German only a few years earlier, was William Shakespeare's *A Midsummer Night's Dream*, a fantasy about fairies, fools, and lovers meeting in an enchanted forest.

Seated side by side in the music room overlooking the woodlands and gardens beyond the glass doors of the conservatory, Felix would try out his ideas on the piano with Fanny adding hers. The music became an overture to *A Midsummer Night's Dream*, one of Felix's most memorable pieces, considered by some critics and composers a new musical style. The quick airy sounds of fairies, of an ass braying, are like a musical painting of the magical forest where the play takes place.

Many years later Felix rewrote the earlier pieces and

devised additional music for the play. His lively wedding march for Titania, queen of the fairies in *A Midsummer Night's Dream*, is often played at marriage ceremonies to this day.

This wonderfully original piece of music was first played as a piano duet by Felix and his sister at a concert in their home in Berlin. It was said that it was this music that first showed signs of Felix's genius. How much input Fanny had in its creation isn't clear, but what seems certain from Fanny's own words was that so long as Felix was living at home he relied on her help and advice. "I have always been his only musical advisor," Fanny proudly wrote about their working together, "and he never writes down a thought before submitting it to my judgment."

At sixteen Felix was ready to have his musical talent judged beyond the safety of family and friends. Music, the thing above all else that he loved, would become his profession.

Abraham Mendelssohn's answer to this idea was a decisive *no*. No one, least of all Fanny, suggested that she also might become a professional composer or performer. With her father so strongly opposed to Felix's ambition, there wasn't a prayer that he would allow his daughter the same choice.

Although fully aware of Felix's talent, Abraham firmly believed that child prodigies, and composers in general, led unhappy lives, that the music world and the public were too unpredictable. Was he thinking of the lives of *wunderkinder*, children like Wolfgang Amadeus Mozart who were paraded in front of royalty as musical novelties and then dismissed or ignored when they grew older? Or was it Beethoven's unhappy life he was thinking of, the details of which he knew all too well? Too often the greatest talents had to bow to the wishes of some rich patrons.

Felix's uncle Jacob Bartholdy agreed that the life of a

professional musician was a sorry one. "It is no career, no life, no aim . . . in the beginning you are just as far as at the end, and as a rule you are even better off at the start than at the end. Let [Felix] go through a regular course of schooling, and then prepare for a state career by studying law at the university."

Fanny, of course, strongly disagreed. It seemed to her that it was her uncle, who lived on inherited wealth, who had no career, no life, and no aim. But there were those outside the family, older musician friends such as Ignaz Moscheles, a composer and one of the foremost interpreters of Beethoven's piano music, who supported Felix against his father and uncle. Both parents were far from overrating their children's talents, claimed Moscheles. "Other prodigies compared to Felix are gifted children, but nothing else. He is a phenomenon."

Still, Abraham remained unconvinced. Felix recalled that his father's angry moods increased the more he seemed bent on a musical career, that whenever he praised Beethoven's works, his father became more unpleasant. As the disagreement continued, others reminded Abraham that several friends of the family, such as Moscheles and Louis Spohr, *had* made successful careers in the music world.

Abraham was finally persuaded to take Felix to Paris to see a respected composer, one named Luigi Cherubini, whom he knew from his stay in that city and whose judgment he did not question. Cherubini was the director of the Paris Music Conservatory in 1825 and one of the most eminent musical figures of his time.

When Felix played his own compositions Cherubini was impressed. He told Abraham that Felix would do well in music, saying, "even now he's doing well." But what he didn't tell Abraham were his doubts about whether Felix had the determination and will to succeed in the music world. He told a friend after the visit that young Felix spends too much money and is too elegantly dressed. Cherubini believed Felix's aristocratic tastes just wouldn't fit the life of a modestly paid musician and composer. In turn, Felix thought little of Cherubini as a composer now well past his prime. At sixteen Felix held strong opinions, especially about good and bad music, and expressed them time and time again in his letters to Fanny. He had little patience with anyone whose judgment he questioned or whose work he considered inferior. To others he appeared arrogant and overconfident, but to Fanny he often admitted to fears and uncertainties about his own work.

In the end Abraham relented, agreed to accept Cherubini's opinion, and offered to help Felix until he became self-supporting. Fanny was delighted and wrote to say how pleased she was about her father's change of heart.

Her father had already made it plain long before this in one of his letters that he would never consider Fanny's music to be anything more than a pleasant pastime. He warned Fanny when she was sixteen that music was never to be "the root of your being and doing."

> Music will perhaps become his profession, whilst for you it can and must only be an ornament . . . We may therefore pardon him some ambition and desire to be acknowledged in a pursuit which appears very important to him . . . while it does you credit that you have always shown yourself good and sensible in these matters; and your very joy at the praise he earns proves that you might, in his place, have merited equal approval.

By his very own words, it's clear that her father recognized Fanny's talent, but his strongly held view of a woman's place within their closed society remained unshakeable. The thought of his daughter becoming a performer, a woman who earned money, was repugnant to him. He could see it no other way—and neither could Lea. Nothing Fanny could do other than leave home (which would have been unthinkable), could have had any effect on this decision. So while Felix would now have their support and encouragement to enter the music world, for Fanny, everything had to remain as before. She could perform at the Berlin Singakademie without pay and entertain friends in their home at 3 Leipziger Strasse, and she could quietly compose her own music so long as it was kept private. Felix's talent would eventually free him from his parents' control. Fanny's talent never would.

While still in Paris Felix wrote to Fanny saying that, in his opinion, the city's reputation as the center of European culture was highly overrated. Although Paris was then the home of such renowned composers as Chopin, Rossini, Meyerbeer, Liszt, and Berlioz, Felix claimed that French music was far below that of the Germans. He was also astounded by Parisians' ignorance of the music of Bach, Mozart, Handel, Haydn, and Beethoven. He complained about Parisian musicians, their pettiness and jealousies, about concertgoers whose manners he said were atrocious.

"When music is being played ladies talk or jump from one chair to the next as if they were playing musical chairs," he told Fanny. "Right in the middle an old gentleman will call out *charmant* while the music is being played."

Fanny, who knew her brother's moods all too well and was amused by his description, cautioned him to be less critical. "You've heard nothing but *salon music* so far [meaning private concerts not open to the public], and the talents are just as trite as here. My son, your letters consist of nothing but criticism . . . if everything were really as bad as you now see it, the trip would be a great loss."

For Fanny, Paris was a special place. She remembered her year-long stay when she was eleven, how she had loved the museums, the Tuilleries Garden, and Parisian life. She still hoped to return to Paris one day.

Tweeking Felix still more she said, "You travel to Paris and hear no decent music, and we stay calmly at home and are forced to stretch our ears," adding that she had just heard Ludwig van Beethoven's Pastoral Symphony for the first time.

A symphony in the 1800s could be heard only in cities supporting a full orchestra and Berlin was one of them. As a Berliner, Fanny was able to hear and enjoy more music than most of her contemporaries, making Fanny's musical knowledge unusual for her day. Some of the works of Bach and Beethoven that Fanny heard were rarely performed because copies of their scores had been lost or forgotten for many years.

Many of Bach's thousands of handwritten scores, for example, would have disappeared completely if it weren't for collectors like Fanny's *tante* Sarah Levy. Fanny's great-aunt rediscovered and collected many original scores, including a copy of one of Bach's grandest works, St. Matthew's Passion, which Felix later reintroduced to the public. Some handwritten sheet music of Johann Sebastian Bach and that of his composer sons were discovered in a German dairy being used to wrap pieces of cheese. Still other unpublished works were found wrapped around tree trunks to protect them from frost.

Not until the 1800s did publishing music and making multiple copies become commonplace. In a time before radio, records, and tapes, concertgoing was the *only* way to hear choral, symphonic, or chamber music. So for the many friends and guests of the Mendelssohns', their private concerts served them well. It brought composers from France such as Franz Liszt and Frédéric Chopin; from Italy, Niccolo Paganini; and German composers, Ignaz Moscheles, Robert Schumann, and Louis Spohr, to Berlin to play their own compositions. This had been a uniquely stimulating atmosphere for both Fanny and her brother.

Felix returned from Paris to complete his formal education at Berlin University, studying geography, history, and esthetics. Though not formally enrolled as a student, Fanny, like other upper-class women of her day, attended occasional lectures at the university, lectures on geography or experimental physics aimed at providing the mostly female audience a smattering of knowledge. Not for another fifty years would women begin to take their place among men in the sciences.

Fanny had a pleasant singing voice, though not as good as her sister Rebecka's, and continued to be a part of the Singakademie chorus, which she had joined as a fifteen-year-old. Being a member made it possible to use the chorus to try out her own choral music, but more often she tested her latest compositions on her audience in the conservatory of their home. These were the only two places she could gauge the reaction of a public audience to her music. Since these were audiences of friends, their criticism would be guarded.

By the time Felix was seventeen he was traveling around Germany with letters of introduction from Herr Zelter, which opened doors to the professional music world. It often resulted in getting invitations to play with well-known musicians, sometimes performing his own piano quartets and concertos.

Now that Felix was rarely home it was up to twenty-year-old Fanny to plan all the Sunday concerts, to rehearse the choir and, several times, to bring in the entire Konigstat orchestra to play orchestral works by Bach, or scenes from a Beethoven opera. In addition, many of Felix's works had their first performance in Berlin under Fanny's supervision. By then she could read a complete orchestral score and know just how the music should sound when played. After each concert Fanny sent back copious notes on how the music was received, and sometimes made suggestions about how Felix's new composition might be improved. She still felt a need to be part of his success, part of his art.

Felix, by then, was traveling a great deal, feasting on a wealth of new music from many parts of Europe. Abraham was very pleased each time news arrived that Felix's appearances as a young concert pianist and composer were well received. His hopes of having a son join his banking firm now rested with his younger son, Paul.

∞ *Chapter 4* ∞

A Suitable Husband

*Women have a difficult task; the constant occupation with apparent
trifles . . . ; the unremitting attention to every detail, the appreciation of every moment and its improvement for some benefit or other
. . . all these and more are the weighty duties of a woman.*
                          Abraham Mendelssohn, March 1828

Abraham and Lea had not yet begun their search for a suitable husband for seventeen-year-old Fanny, one who would
give her financial security and who would fit within their
closed circle of relatives and friends, when Fanny met an
aspiring painter named Wilhelm Hensel.

The first in a string of problems, as seen by Fanny's parents, was that Wilhelm Hensel came from a different class of
German society. The second was that there was as yet no
proof that he could earn a living from his paintings, though
he showed promise of becoming an excellent painter.

Wilhelm Hensel was the son of a poor country minis-
ter who, by his own efforts, had become an artist. From
early childhood, with no formal training and no way of
obtaining even the most basic materials, young Wilhelm
learned to draw and paint. He used all his spare time to
gather materials for making his own colors out of fruits,
leaves, and roots, for there were no paint boxes in Linum,
Germany, where he grew up. Like Felix, he knew at an early
age what he wanted to do. In his case, it was to paint. And
just as Abraham was doubtful of Felix pursuing a musical
career, so Wilhelm's parents discouraged him from becom-

25

Wilhelm
Hensel

ing an artist. They urged him to study something that would give him a secure income, for his parents could neither continue supporting him nor leave him any inheritance. So, with a heavy heart, he decided to become a mining engineer, all the while devoting every free moment to drawing and painting.

By pure luck an art critic, seeing one of his pictures, urged him to give up engineering and study art. He also offered to help support Wilhelm during his first few years, but the help he received was so small that having enough to live on was a constant source of worry. As head of his household, for by then his father was dead, Wilhelm needed to provide for others besides himself. Obligations to his family forced him to take any kind of artwork that would pay him some money. He reluctantly put aside his first love, painting, to illustrate inexpensive books and almanacs, working long hours by candlelight in unheated rooms.

At the outbreak of the Napoleonic Wars, in 1811, Wilhelm enlisted as a volunteer. By a stroke of good fortune, he found himself in Paris at the war's end, and remained there to study art. He later traveled to Italy to study the works of the old masters, and his technique as a painter greatly improved.

Wilhelm's greatest ambition was to become a court painter for some German nobleman when he returned to his own country. During the early nineteenth century photography, which had only recently been invented, was not widely in use. Instead, portrait painters and landscape artists were hired by the nobles, wealthy merchants, and bankers to record on canvas their family, their homes, and their possessions. Some of the most beautiful portraits in Europe were made by "court painters."

Though he never achieved the title of "court painter," talent and a dogged persistence did win Hensel many commissions to paint portraits of the nobility. At the height of his career he traveled to London to paint the portraits of Queen Victoria and her husband, Prince Albert. That same persistence was to win him his wife.

At their first meeting, Wilhelm was immediately attracted to young Fanny, to her genuine interest in art and to her expressive, vivacious face. Fanny and her mother had gone to see an exhibit of Wilhelm's drawings. This set of drawings had won him a scholarship from the Prussian government to study in Rome.

His art also impressed Lea Mendelssohn, who invited Wilhelm to the Mendelssohn home to make sketches of the family and many of their nearest friends before leaving for Rome. As a result, he was a constant visitor at 3 Leipziger Strasse. Fanny was impressed with his talent and became fond of this admiring young man. And Hensel, it seems, fell in love with Fanny, perhaps long before she was aware of it, for it would have been surprising if they were ever alone together for more than a few minutes.

After leaving Berlin, Wilhelm wrote a warm, romantic letter to Fanny asking her to marry him when he returned from Rome. The letter, to his dismay, was answered forcefully and somewhat sternly by Fanny's mother instead of Fanny. In the formal manner of her day she wrote:

> Seriously, dear Mr. Hensel, you must not be angry with me because I cannot allow a correspondence between you and Fanny. Put yourself in fairness, for one moment in the place of a mother, and exchange your interests for mine and my refusal will appear natural, just, and sensible . . . you are probably now violently denouncing [my behavior] as most barbaric. For the same reason that makes me forbid an engagement, I must declare myself against any correspondence.

She went on to explain that although she had no objection to him personally, the difference in their ages (Wilhelm was eleven years older than Fanny) caused her some concern. Also, she said, the uncertainty of his position troubled her.

Her reason is made even clearer in the next sentence: "An artist so long as he is single, is a happy being." But, after marriage, "when domestic cares take hold, the magic disappears."

Here, then, was her real concern for her daughter, unused to worries about money or her place in society.

Lea softened her message by saying she made it a point to give her children what she considered "simple and unpretentious habits," so they need not look for rich marriages; but . . . "a moderate but fixed income are necessary conditions for a happy life. Rest assured that we will not be against you when, at the end of your studies, you can satisfy us about your position. . . . Fanny is very young, and, Heaven be praised, has . . . had no concern and no passion. I will not have you, by love letters, transport her for years into a state of consuming passion."

Fanny, to be sure, was not consulted on any of this and it's possible she only saw her mother's letter after she married. Her mother's description of her having no concern and no passion was not true when applied to music, and by extension, to her brother, Felix. It was true that even modest flirtations with young men or any outward signs of adolescent daydreaming seemed not to be part of Fanny's life. Whom she would eventually marry would be left to her parents in any case. Romance, for Fanny, appeared as forbidden as laziness and self-indulgence. Marriage would come "when it was time." And the time was then at least five years away.

Wilhelm continued to send letters from Italy addressed to Lea Mendelssohn, who read them to her daughter. This allowed her mother a subtle kind of censorship. To Fanny, he was only permitted to send sketches from his notebooks. During the five years Wilhelm was in Italy, they did not see each other at all since he could not afford the trip from Rome to Berlin.

When he returned in the fall of 1828, Wilhelm needed to work out a new relationship with Fanny and her family, for changes had taken place in both Wilhelm, now thirty-three, and Fanny, a woman of twenty-two. She was no longer the modest seventeen-year-old he had left five years earlier. Fanny's parents had still not decided if he was a suitable husband. Wilhelm still had neither a secure position, money, nor established a name for himself as a painter. Their response to him was sometimes less than welcoming, which made him unhappy but no less persistent.

Hensel found himself becoming jealous of Fanny's extreme attachment to her family, especially to her brother, seeing in him a rival for her attention and heart. On the other side, it was hard for Fanny to appreciate the struggle her would-be fiancé had overcome to achieve his goal. What she did understand, though, was his dedication to his art. Would he, in turn, understand *her* attachment to music, she needed to know, and by extension, her attachment to Felix?

Having lived her life until now without any romantic love, most of her strong feelings had focused on her brother who was living the life she would have wanted for herself.

Hensel, sensing this, had to assure Fanny that he would not object to her closeness to Felix, that in fact he was also fond of him. In Fanny's diary, kept until her death, she wrote: "Hensel brought the sketch of Felix's portrait, which shows a clear and beautiful conception. Felix himself is quite charmed with it, and I fancy he feels very different toward Hensel since the portrait was begun." Felix, like his parents, surely must have wondered how a marriage with this rather stern-looking older man would turn out. Hensel knew little about music. What would this mean for Fanny?

Fanny herself didn't know.

In a letter to Felix she wrote: "Solve this riddle for me . . . as Hensel mentioned you today in relation to me, I know that he loves me because he respects my love for you." She often called Wilhelm by his last name.

Fanny was finally fully convinced that Wilhelm would support her as an artist, that unlike her father he could see the deep need she had for her music. She felt sure that Felix's and Wilhelm's need to express their creative instinct was the bond that would hold all three together.

The engagement was announced in January 1829, more than a year after Hensel's return from Italy. During most of that year Felix was in England, a frequent guest conductor and piano soloist of the London Symphony Orchestra, performing his own works and those of the German composers he loved. His new compositions were greeted with lavish praise, making his name better known in Britain than in his own country.

A month before the wedding Hensel sent Felix several portrait etchings he'd made of friends and family members. While praising Hensel for the excellent likenesses of most of the portraits, Felix was quite critical of Fanny's. He said that although the portrait of her was beautiful, he didn't like it. He explained that even though it was splendidly drawn, and strikingly lifelike, it was the pose, dress, and facial expression which, he said, "failed to capture her rapturous quality, her enthusiasm. It is not so much on the surface as within. Don't take it amiss, my good court painter, but I have known my sister longer than you have."

The only portraits ever made of Fanny were by her husband in the formal manner of that period. It would have taken a good modern photographer to catch the qualities Felix felt were missing, or the skill of a Rembrandt.

Fanny couldn't wait for Felix's return to Berlin. He assured her that he would certainly be back in time for her wedding and promised to bring with him a short organ composition written especially for the occasion. Dashing off a letter to him before his planned departure, Fanny sent a long description of the early wedding preparations.

> Beckchen [Rebecka] is embroidering now, Hensel is sketching, and Mother is reading the paper. . . . Our furnishings are ready, and very lovely: extremely taste-ful, suitable and nice. . . . My dowry is ready and I think my outfit will please you. . . . On Wednesday, there will be a small display of my dowry and the girls will stream in to see it. Friday Hensel will move his things in, and Saturday, there will be a big com-motion. The crown ceremony begins around 1:00.

Felix received the letter at the end of an incredibly suc-cessful tour of the British Isles which established him as a remarkably talented young composer. He was, at age twenty, also one of Europe's youngest conductors. After being away for almost a year on a demanding performing sched-ule, conducting and composing new works, he was ready to come home for a much needed rest. But at the end of his stay in London he was hit by a horse-drawn carriage and seriously injured his kneecap. Unable to leave his bed for two months because of the injury, it became impossible for him to attend Fanny's wedding, to his and Fanny's bitter disappointment.

The day of her wedding Fanny sent Felix a very emo-tional letter. It was almost as if she needed Felix to help her cross into this new phase of her life, that she needed his blessings on her marriage as she needed them on her music. Felix was still her "twin," her *other self*.

"I have your portrait before me, and ever repeating your dear name, and thinking of you as if you stood by my side, I weep!"

The organ music Felix wanted to send as a wedding gift was left unfinished. Felix complained in his letter that not only his knee was damaged but also his power of concentration. Instead, Fanny composed a short piece for the ceremony herself.

It wasn't until December, two months after the wedding, that Felix recovered enough to make the journey to Berlin in time for his parents' silver wedding anniversary party. In April, Felix left the Mendelssohn home for a long journey on the European continent—and never again returned to 3 Leipziger Strasse to stay.

Garden House at
3 Leipziger Strasse

∞ *Chapter 5* ∞

Only an Ornament

*You will not misunderstand me when I tell you that Felix's success
has neither surprised, dazzled, nor confounded me.*

Fanny Mendelssohn, June 1829

Shortly after she married, Fanny wrote, "My husband has
given me the duty of going to the piano every morning
immediately after breakfast, because interruptions occur
later on. He came over this morning and silently laid the
paper [with one of his poems] on the piano . . . five minutes
later I called him over and sang it to him."

Fanny in turn was a great support to her husband,
helping him with financial matters, offering him a secure
and pleasant place to work. The garden house at 3 Leipziger
Strasse was converted into a home for the newlyweds, with a
studio added for Hensel and an adjacent music room for
Fanny. Though lovely in spring and summer, the glass-
enclosed rooms were unbearably cold and drafty in winter, a
complaint she only admitted to in a letter written seventeen
years later. Fanny was to live in the garden house the rest of
her life.

The thought of visiting warm and sunny Italy became
more and more attractive to the couple as winter ap-
proached and so plans were made to go as soon as it could
be arranged.

Wilhelm not only looked forward to sharing with his young bride all the places he loved, but secretly wished he could start a German Academy of Art in Italy similar to one already established by the French. Fanny was equally excited about the trip and the chance to see things she had only experienced through her husband's sketches and the letters he'd written to her mother. Besides, Felix would also be spending time traveling in Italy that same year. The thought of being together again with Felix delighted her. So it was with much disappointment that their travel plans had to be canceled when Fanny learned she was pregnant.

Instead, it was Felix who made the grand tour of Europe for the next two years, visiting all the important cities of Austria, Switzerland, Britain, and Italy. Once again Fanny would only *read* about Italian opera, Italian scenery, Italian charm as she had for years when Hensel was there.

Letters from Rome, Vienna, Stuttgart, London, Edinburgh, wherever Felix was staying, came as regularly as a weekly news report despite his heavy schedule of performing. The letters that passed between brother and sister not only contained the usual family news but all the music gossip: what concerts they heard, the music they liked or didn't. Paganini, considered to this day one of the world's great violinists, both dazzled and delighted Fanny with his concert in Berlin. Fanny, describing her excitement on hearing Paganini perform, said he "played with the frenzy and energy of the devil . . . ripping the heart out of the poor violin."

At the same time, Felix was dazzling the British with his new music inspired both by Shakespeare's plays and by Welsh and Scottish scenery. His *Midsummer Night's Dream* overture, music for *The Tempest*, the Hebrides Overture (a musical portrayal of the dramatic landscapes of the western islands off Scotland), and the Scottish Symphony, were popular from their first performance. He was accepted at the highest levels of British society, invited to play for Queen Victoria, and, as an honored guest at parties and balls, courted and flattered. In turn, Felix loved being in Britain and wrote glowing letters home about the beauty of London, the Scottish Highlands, Wales, and the country-side. His only complaints were about the folk music he heard.

> Anything but national music! May ten devils take all folklore. Here I am in Wales, and oh how lovely! A harpist sits in the lobby of every Inn playing . . . dreadful, vulgar, fake stuff. . . . It's enough to drive one crazy, it's even given me a toothache.

On and on went the tirade about bagpipes, Welsh harps, hurdy-gurdies, and shrill, nasal voices accompanied by bumbling fingers. Obviously Felix's training as a classical composer had made him deaf to this kind of folk music. Fanny would probably have agreed, for her taste and training were the same as his.

Some of Felix's popularity with concertgoers in England came from the number of works by Bach and Beethoven he introduced to his British audiences, works they had never heard before. His audiences, as in all public concerts, varied from those who truly loved music to those who came to be seen and to see friends. If the music played was new to them, as it often was, their response could range from angry disapproval to shouts of praise. But Felix was fortunate, his own romantic-style music was popular, as were the German compositions he chose.

Cherubini noted that Felix showed a remarkable degree of self-confidence at age sixteen, which only grew after his public acclaim by the age of twenty. Even so, Felix had a moment of panic just before a performance at one of his early concerts in a large concert hall. Due to a last-minute mix-up, he found himself seated in front of a new grand piano he hadn't had time to try out. As he was about to play and the hall filled with ladies in gaily decorated hats, he began to panic. Because of "the fearful heat . . . the unknown instrument, and up to the moment when I went on I felt exceedingly nervous, I think even feverish. But," he wrote, "the gay bonnets gave me a nice reception and applauded when I came in [and] I lost all my timidity."

To his amusement, he saw the colorful bonnets moving in time with his music, which he likened in his letter to the wind blowing over a tulip bed.

Some of the publicity about Felix's successful concerts set off a family crisis. Fanny, hoping to act as a buffer between her father and Felix, sent a hurried letter warning her brother of an "unpleasant matter" concerning their father. Abraham had noticed that in several English newspapers his son was named Felix *Mendelssohn* (leaving off *Bartholdy*).

> I know and approve of your intention to lay aside someday this name that *we dislike*, [wrote Fanny,] but you can't do it yet because you're a minor [Felix was not yet twenty-one] and it's not necessary to make you aware of the unpleasant consequences it could have for you. You distress Father by your actions.

Rebecka, Fanny's younger sister, often signed her letters Mendelssohn *meden* Bartholdy, *meden* being the Greek word for *never*. Both sisters felt a sense of loyalty to their grandfather's name and reputation. Their dislike for the uncle who adopted the name Bartholdy and who was opposed to Felix's decision to make music his career, added to their distaste. Fanny recommended that Felix, if questioned, should say the omission of Bartholdy was a newspaper error. And to calm Felix when he received his father's angry letter, she reminded him that their father's words always sounded harsher than they were meant to be.

> You know how it always used to upset you when our parents concealed their satisfaction from you. Father makes us upset the same way when he appears so indifferent and stoic, but then we'll catch him reading your letters three or four times and telling people how happy he is about everything you do. Only we're not supposed to know it.

Abraham did write his son a long letter repeating his reasons for adopting the name Bartholdy, ending with the statement that "there can no more be a Christian [named] *Mendelssohn* than there can be a Jewish *Confucius.* If Mendelssohn is your name, you are ipso facto a Jew. And this, if for no other reason than because it is contrary to fact [because Felix was baptized as a boy], can be of no benefit to you. Dear Felix, take this to heart and act accordingly."

Felix's reply came a month later telling Fanny how grateful he was for her letter, grateful even though the letter was unnecessary. "It would never in my life occur to me to want to oppose Father's will. No, believe me, it doesn't enter my mind and I think there should be few misunderstandings . . . that won't be easy to clear up." Nevertheless, the single name *Mendelssohn* became as commonly used then as it is now. But Felix was careful to sign his letters home as Felix M.B.

For some time, Felix had been publishing his musical compositions. In fact, he was pursued by music companies anxious to print his music. When, in 1827 and 1830, a collection of twenty-four songs for voice and piano were published, six of them were actually by Fanny even though all were listed under her brother's name alone. The reason for this dishonorable act toward a sister for whom Felix felt such love and affection is hard to understand today. Fanny could hardly have been considered a competitor after Felix's career had become so successful. If Fanny had been asked, and there's no evidence that she was, would she have agreed to this use of her music? Whatever her inner feelings might have been, deference to her father, brother, and husband was the rule by which she lived.

While Felix did not hesitate to admit to anyone who praised one of Fanny's songs, as Queen Victoria did, that his sister wrote it, as far as the world in general knew, the songs were all his.

From the beginning, Felix showed himself unwilling to fight on his sister's behalf in her efforts to be recognized as a serious artist. He offered her warm personal praise in his letters or when he was with her, but that was all. He had no stomach for rebellion, nor did he seem to question his society's rules on the place of women. If Felix ever felt any guilt about taking credit for her songs, it was never expressed.

Abraham's strong opposition to having Fanny's music published seems illogical today. Being a published composer did not mean a disruption of one's family life as it did for a performing artist. Was it to prevent the impression that her husband could not provide sufficient support? Or perhaps to prevent the label of "professional" at a time when it carried little prestige for women? Or was it to protect Fanny from critics who did not take women's musical works seriously?

In less than a year after her marriage, Fanny gave birth to a little boy. The baby was two months premature and was, at first, not expected to live. Little Sebastian was Fanny's and Wilhelm's only child.

When a letter announcing the birth caught up with Felix, who was still on tour, he wrote:

> Oh my little sister, I know everything! Just received a letter of the 16th which contained much about Sebastian and they are congratulating me on being an uncle. . . . Send me everything relating to all this: cards, cut-out newspaper articles, if possible even his baby rattle . . . I wish you would also give him the name Felix; the name does have something pretty about it, after all, and I think later I might really love the little rascal if he carried my name—otherwise not.

The baby, in fact, was named after Johann Sebastian Bach, still Fanny's favorite composer.

It was by then a well-established family custom to send a piece of music for every sort of family celebration. Felix planned to send a song in honor of his new little nephew, but said the song turned out badly, "just as milk stirred too long turns into cheese." Despite the apology he sent it the next day.

For Fanny's birthday, a year later, Felix delighted her by sending a Sebastian Bach organ piece she had not heard before, saying it sounded as if one were listening to the angels in heaven singing. From time to time Fanny mailed Felix one of her own musical compositions, eager for his opinion and comments about her work. The tables had now been turned, for now Felix was *her* only advisor and best critic.

After the birth of Sebastian, the close living arrangements at 3 Leipziger Strasse added to Fanny's duties as a daughter, sister, and mother. Rebecka was now also married and living in the main house with her parents. She later had five children. With their father often away on business, with family illnesses, and frequent visitors, there was less time for the "luxury" of playing music. And even less time for composing. When she complained to Felix that she now had lost all inspiration for new music, his reply was not very sympathetic, not the kind of response she had hoped for.

> You can hardly expect a man like me to wish you some musical ideas; it is just greediness for you to complain of a scarcity of them . . . if you wanted to, you would already be composing with might and main and if you do not want to, why do you fret so? If I had a child to nurse, then I would not want to write scores (!) . . . But seriously, the child is not even half a year old, and you already want to think of ideas other than Sebastian? (not Bach). Be happy that you have him. Music fails to appear only when it has no place.

Even so, Fanny's devotion to music, combined with a will to never make music *just an ornament*, prodded her to keep working to improve her piano playing. She studied all of Felix's latest compositions and continued to arrange for their performance whenever possible. Quietly and persistently she started composing again, music that only her Berliner friends and family would hear. By the end of her life, she had written over four hundred compositions, an impressive number for any artist, and for a woman of her day, truly amazing. The number and range of her compositions might even have surprised her brother, for she only showed him the select few that she was most proud of.

In 1837, at age twenty-eight, Felix quietly married the beautiful Cecile Jeanrenaud in the city of Frankfurt, a mere half-day's journey from Berlin, and only introduced her to his family eight months after their wedding. She was the perfect adoring wife, who would devote her life to Felix and their children. The fact that neither Fanny nor his parents were at the wedding was another sign of Felix's detachment from his family and the control they once had on his life.

By the time he was thirty-three Felix had had enough of constant travel and settled in the city of Leipzig, Germany, with his wife and three small children. There he was appointed director of the concert hall called the Gewandhaus, whose orchestra had the reputation of being one of the best in Germany. Besides his duties as director and his outpouring of new musical compositions, he still concertized in Britain and elsewhere from time to time. But visits between brother and sister almost ceased.

> Things are different now [wrote Fanny] from when we used to sit together at home and you showed me a totally new musical idea without telling me its purpose . . . on the second day another idea would come, and on the third you would undergo the torment of working them out. And I was there to comfort you when you thought you couldn't write anything more. But those lovely times are a thing of the past.

Fanny's letters now took on a mildly scolding tone, faulting her brother for not even sending his finished scores. When she heard that he had completed his new Reformation Symphony, she asked petulantly, "When will I get to hear it?" Fanny's habit of going over every new work, line by line, saying what parts she liked and didn't like, was perhaps what kept Felix from sending her his new compositions before they were performed. Though letters were exchanged as before, his music came only rarely. Fanny grew increasingly hurt and disappointed that Felix went his own way with little or no help from her.

Venice,
Italy

Chapter 6

Italy, at Last!

How can anything be pleasing after a year-long stay in Italy?
Felix Mendelssohn, October 1840

Now, ten years after their canceled plans to visit Italy, the Hensels prepared for an extensive Italian vacation to savor and enjoy its beauty, music, and art. Traveling by horse-driven coach through the German Alps into Switzerland, thirty-four-year-old Fanny, her husband, and nine-year-old Sebastian arrived in Italy in December of 1839. Italy charmed her from the first but it was the city of Venice with its "fairy-like beauty," its many canals, gondolas, and the open squares, called *piazzas* in Italian, that she found so totally enchanting.

> I do not remember in my whole life having felt so much astonishment, admiration, emotion, and joy in any twenty-four hours as I have in this wonderful city. . . . Here in the piazza there's a permanent fair spiced with quarrels, shouting vendors, and singing. Nothing but the sight of shirts and aprons prosaically hanging out to dry . . . could convince you that you are not dreaming.

While Venice's exhilarating atmosphere made Fanny feel freer than she'd ever felt before, Rome provided something more. It was there that Fanny found the admiring public she so badly missed at home. Rome, Fanny told her family, was a mixture of serenity and excitement. "I was very spoiled on the trip by an exceedingly grateful public that continually urged and invited me to play this and that, and always kept me on my toes. One became accustomed to that only too quickly," she wrote.

Italy was like a magnet that attracted painters, singers, musicians, and actors to its cities, and a place where operas were more popularly supported than anywhere else. Renaissance sculptures filled public squares, and paintings and frescoes covered the walls and ceilings of churches and palaces.

In the heart of the Italian capital the French had established a school for art and music called the French Academy. Its members, both painters and musicians, included the well-known painter Jean-Auguste Ingres. It was there that Fanny met a group of lively young musicians, and one who was destined to become one of France's outstanding composers, Charles Gounod. He wrote about his impressions of Fanny in his memoirs years later, calling Madame Hensel "a musician beyond comparison, a remarkable pianist, and a woman of superior mind." Describing her as small and thin in person but "with an energy that showed itself in her deep eyes and in her fiery glance," he said she was a gifted composer. It was this recognition that Fanny desired most and heard the least. By 1840, she had been composing music for almost twenty years. Gounod's recollection continues:

> M. and Mme. Hensel came to the Academy on Sunday evenings. She [played] . . . with the grace and simplicity of those who make music because they love it . . . thanks to her fine talent and prodigious memory,

I was brought to the knowledge of a mass of German musical masterpieces *of which I was completely ignorant at that time* . . . pieces by Johann Sebastian Bach—and several Mendelssohn compositions which were also a revelation to me from an unknown world.

Fanny, looking back on this happy time, how it had affected her music and her view of life itself, had only the happiest memories. Italy had lived up to all her expectations.

"When I think back on Rome as I often do, and recall how gloriously we lived there and how much I'd like to return for a longer stay, I must immediately keep in mind that then I wouldn't be able to see you any longer," she wrote Felix. "So you can't have your cake and eat it, too!"

But, in fact, by this time visits between Fanny and Felix were few and far between. Occasionally Fanny traveled to Leipzig to attend a concert or visit with Felix's wife and small children, Karl, Marie, and Paul, but visits were always brief now that her father had died, and Fanny had taken on the responsibility of caring for her aging mother. Once or twice Felix stopped in Berlin on his way to some other city. The nagging feeling that she was left out of his thoughts and life, when he never was from hers, made her sad.

In 1840, when she turned thirty-five, she wrote, "Whoever might doubt that ten years is a long time need only read letters that were written then. It's dreadful how few of the people and relationships mentioned in them remain." Her father died at age fifty-nine, as suddenly as his own father had, without any sign of illness. Their uncle Jacob Bartholdy and several of their aunts were also dead by then.

In Fanny's letters to Felix she continued saying how happy she was that they happened to be siblings. But in a rare sign of anger and frustration she also said, "My God,

I'd love to be proud of my brother, with all my satisfaction, if only I could get around to it. Obviously I'm proud of you among strangers." Then, scolding Felix for the little time they had spent together in the past ten years except for "a few days stolen in haste," she wrote, "this will very likely continue for the rest of our lives."

What was Fanny implying when she wrote that she would like to be proud of him with all her satisfaction and pleasure? Was it a deep hurt because of the nearly total separation from the "twin" who had filled her early years and the fear that this situation would not change?

A piano composition called *Das Jahr*, German for *The Year*, was written by Fanny a year after she returned to Berlin. It was inspired by the places in Italy she had seen and loved: Naples, Amalfi, Pompeii, Venice, and most of all, Rome. This set of musical pieces was one of her most ambitious works. The twelve parts (named after each month of the year) began with January, subtitled "A Dream," with its subdued tones for a stormy month, and was followed by a livelier, lighter February, the month of carnivals in Rome. The music for March included religious themes for the Easter season, and continued into December, the month of "renewed hope."

Fanny believed Italy had a profound effect on her, that the praise and admiration she found there gave her greater confidence to continue to compose.

Although written in 1840, *Das Jahr* was not published until recently. A rough draft of the music resides in the Mendelssohn archives in the Prussian State Library in Berlin. Another copy illustrated by her husband remains within the family.

∞ *Chapter 7* ∞

"Considering the Composer
Is a Woman"

*Limburger said you should be a touring artist, that you would play
circles around the others.*

Felix Mendelssohn, November 1835

*I*t may have been affection for his sister that prompted Felix
to tell Fanny he agreed with his friend Jakob Limburger, a
member of the Gewandhaus concert directorship, that she
would play circles around other (professional) pianists. Or
it may have been meant to assure her, as her father always
had, that he still admired her talent.

Besides Limburger's complimentary comment, the
British music critic, Henry F. Chorley, called Fanny "an
amateur pianist and composer of no ordinary force and
feeling." Despite his use of the label "amateur," based on his
definition of the word to mean an unpaid performer, his
praise was sincere. He then added in the same article that
had Fanny been a poor man's daughter, she would have taken
her place in the music world alongside such admired pianists
as Clara Schumann and Marie Pleyel, two women musicians
of the very highest order. Clearly, he saw that a woman's
place in music was determined not only by talent but also
by her economic status.

Charles Horsley, Felix's student and the son of an
English composer, first heard Fanny play at a farewell party

Robert and
Clara Schumann

given in his honor in Leipzig. Fanny, Felix, and Clara Schumann all performed on the same program. Horsely remarked that Fanny played magnificently, with much of her brother's fire and style. Fanny's former teacher, using a somewhat similar comparison, had once described her musicianship as "playing like a man."

Clara Wieck Schumann and Marie Pleyel were among the best European pianists of their day. Marie Pleyel's husband was a composer and maker of pianofortes. Clara Schumann had started performing as a child and continued to do so all her life. Clara's mother had been a student of Fredrick Wieck before her marriage to him and was a soloist in the Leipzig Concert Hall before Clara was born. There was never a doubt in her father's mind that Clara would someday become a first-rate pianist.

Clara's early talent, like Mozart's and his sister's, was carefully developed by her father, a demanding, authoritarian man who insisted that all his five children become pianists. Only Clara showed real promise. Since her parents divorced when she was only five and her father was awarded custody of his daughter, her life became totally dictated by his will. At twelve Clara began her concert tours, partly to satisfy her father's ego, partly to earn money for the family. Her father acted as her business manager until her marriage to the composer, Robert Schumann. The money she earned was to be put in trust for her until she grew older but, in fact, was never given to Clara. She continued to perform long after her marriage and all during her numerous pregnancies. By the time her husband died in 1856, she had given birth to eight children. Left with only a tiny income, she gave hundreds of concerts in order to support her family.

Clara had little confidence in her talent as a composer, though she wrote numerous songs and piano works during her lifetime. Neither her father nor her composer husband gave her encouragement to be anything other than a concert pianist. Mainly she used her talent to promote her husband's music instead of her own. For most of their lives, her children were cared for by nannies or went to boarding schools while she traveled. Whatever conflict resulted from her duties as a mother and her music were usually settled in favor of her music. After her husband was confined to a mental institution, her need to earn money was her primary duty, but playing music was as important to her as food and sleep. But for her success as a pianist, Clara's life would have been a tragic one.

With Fanny, there was no economic necessity to perform, no pushing parent. Accepting the arduous life of a performing artist would have meant relying on the help of her father or husband to both manage the business of concertizing and to be her constant travel companion. It would have been an impossible request to make of either of them.

No middle- or upper-class woman would expect to travel by herself in Europe in the 1800s. Travel could be, and often was, physically exhausting. On Felix's first trip to London, for example, he spent three additional seasick days on board a ship anchored outside London harbor unable to enter the Thames River during a storm. Traveling by coach on rough, unpaved roads could be equally demanding. Today, a trip by plane from Paris to London takes only one hour.

For Madame Pleyel, Anna de Belleville, and Marie Blahetka, all brilliant concert performers in the 1800s, the effort was too great. They gave up careers on the concert stage after they married because of the stress of combining a professional life with family life. Only Clara Schumann persisted, playing over one thousand three hundred public programs in her lifetime.

. . .

Clara's husband, Robert, and Felix were good friends. Together they established the first German music school in 1843 in Leipzig, where they both taught piano and composition.

When Clara Schumann visited Berlin, she was a guest of the Mendelssohns and attended several of Fanny's Sunday recitals. Though well aware of each other's talent, and both outstanding women pianists, they never became friends. Clara, already famous throughout Europe and the younger of the two, was competitive and dismissive toward other women pianists. In turn, Fanny's reserve may have prevented her from pursuing a friendship that appeared unwelcomed. It seems, therefore, that neither made the effort. Fanny knew that on several occasions Felix had performed duo-piano music with Clara Schumann on stage and arranged innumerable appearances for her at the Gewandhaus Concert Hall where he was director. She may well have been jealous of Clara's association with her brother, and Clara was probably envious of Fanny's wealth.

Fanny was also aware of and perhaps a bit jealous of Felix's friendship with the singer Jenny Lind, known as "The Swedish Nightingale," for whom he tried to write an opera. She, too, had given numerous concerts under Felix's direction, particularly in Britain.

As director of a concert hall Felix could easily have arranged to bring his sister's music before the public, but he did this only once, including one of Fanny's songs in his program. To both praise and then ignore his own sister's music was an inconsistency he did not seem to recognize and Fanny never challenged.

Ironically, it can almost be said that Felix supported women in music more than most men of his time. Early in his career he met a young woman composer named

Josephine Lang when she was fifteen. Josephine, born ten years after Fanny, also came from a musical family. Her father was a court musician, her mother an opera singer. Felix, who praised her early attempts at composing, visited her every day for several months in 1830 and 1831 giving her free lessons in fugues, counterpoint, and theory, offering her more encouragement than he did his own sister. Both Fanny and Josephine composed romantic songs and piano pieces, but it was Lang not Fanny who received the attention, praise, and publicity for her music.

Josephine Lang was lucky to receive the personal help of a male contemporary, for at the time women were not accepted into music conservatories to study theory and composition and had to work under the guidance of a family member or tutor. Most women studied to become either singers or soloists on piano or a stringed instrument. They were not asked to perform in or conduct a professional orchestra, nor did any of them manage concert halls where they could have tried out their own compositions. So, while effectively preventing women from receiving the same encouragement or opportunities to compose large works, the music world of the 1800s dismissed women's music as light and insubstantial. Also typical were comments by male critics that began with these dismissive words: "considering the composer is a woman . . ."

This same attitude toward women persisted in the literary world as well. For example, in order to see her novels published in nineteenth-century Britain, Mary Ann Evans took the pen name George Elliot. And in France George Sand, born Aurore Dupin, published her first books, which she coauthored with Jules Sandeau, under his name. When Jules became ill and could no longer write, Aurore adopted a man's name in order to compete in the literary world of France. Other women wrote from a need to use their creative talents, whether or not their work would ever be published, as did the American poet Emily Dickinson. In music, Fanny was the same. Most of her work remains unpublished even to this day. Her reputation during her lifetime was for her virtuoso piano playing, which received the praise of such renowned composers as Franz Liszt, Ignaz Mosheles, and Charles Gounod.

At the Singakademie rehearsals and in preparing her Sunday concerts Fanny suffered the nagging frustration that bedeviled nonprofessionals who had to "make do" with less than professional performers and too little rehearsal time.

"Recently I've been rehearsing and performing a great deal of music," wrote Fanny. "If only *once* I could have as many rehearsals as I wanted! I really believe I have the talent for working out pieces and making the interpretation clear to people. But oh, the *dilettantes!*"

To be sure, some of the singers and musicians who performed Fanny's compositions were not professionals, but without them she would have had no way at all to test her music on an audience. She herself suffered from the label *dilettante,* however unfair it seems today. But aside from the care she gave her immediate family, she put all her energy into her music and into making the Sunday concerts as polished as possible.

It happened at one of her Sunday performances, after playing the piano, that Fanny was asked, or rather pushed into conducting the Konigstat orchestra hired for the concert. The conductor had accidentally smashed his fingers before coming to the Mendelssohn home and was having trouble directing the music, one of Fanny's pieces. Turning toward Fanny, he strode over and handed her his baton, the little white stick Felix is said to have introduced to the music world, and insisted she take over. "Had I not been so horribly shy, and embarrassed . . . I would have been able to conduct reasonably well," said Fanny. "It was great fun to hear my own piece for the first time in two years, and find everything the way I had remembered." The piece, an overture, had only been performed once, since playing it required a full orchestra.

Later the conductor again handed back the baton and urged her to take over the rest of the concert. "People seemed to like it," she said modestly. It was a most unexpected pleasure.

Fanny Mendelssohn Hensel became one of the few women, if not the *only* woman, to conduct a full orchestra in the mid-1800s.

Chapter 8

"I Cannot Say That I Approve"

Fanny has neither inclination nor vocation for authorship. She is too much all that a woman ought to be for this.

Felix Mendelssohn, June 1837

$\mathcal{A}$braham Mendelssohn described himself in his later years as a *hyphen* or a mere *link* between two generations and two famous men, his father and his son. As a financier he was certainly not an unimportant link, for he provided the financial support for his son's early success. But for Fanny her father could be described as the brackets that enclosed her world. Only after his death did she begin to assert herself as an artist, and even then with misgivings. In 1836, when she was thirty-one, a year after his death, she sent off an anguished note to her brother telling him she felt "like a donkey between two bales of hay." While her husband encouraged her to publish her music she knew that Felix was still opposed to it. "I would of course comply totally with the wishes of my husband in any other matter, yet on this issue alone it's crucial to have your consent for without it I might not do anything of the kind."

A year earlier Fanny wrote Felix, "I'm so unreasonably afraid of you anyway (and of no other person, except slightly of Father), that I actually never play particularly well in front of you."

Cécile
Jeanrenaud

Charles
Gounod

Karl
Klingemann

Niccolò
Paganini

The ever widening gap between Felix's musical accomplishments and hers, his reliance on friends and not on her for advice, had a curious effect on Fanny. Doubts about her own talent made her cling even harder to her now-famous brother, placing Felix in an uncomfortable position. Fanny's begging letter seeking advice was a plea for help. In her mind her brother seemed to take on the authority of a parent. And, in fact, Felix did just this by withholding his approval. Any modest success by his sister could no longer have been the slightest threat to Felix. Real rivalry between them had ceased fifteen years earlier. Her brother's lack of encouragement to publish her music was a terrible blow.

Early in 1837, Fanny had a single song published in a collection of songs, a copy of which she sent to Felix. This was the one song he had performed at the Gewandhaus Concert Hall.

> I must write you about your song yesterday. How beautiful it was! I felt so strange when I began, your soft symphony imitating the waves, with all the people listening in perfect silence; but never did the song please me better. . . . The people understood it and gave it much applause when it was over. I thank you in the name of the public of Leipzig and elsewhere for publishing it against my wish.

A more puzzling statement would be hard to imagine. Yet, that same year in response to his mother's letter begging Felix to encourage Fanny to publish her music, he objected again. In his long reply, though full of words of affection for Fanny, his answer was sure to make her unhappy.

> You write to me about Fanny's new compositions, and say that I ought to persuade her to publish them. Your

praise is, quite unnecessary . . . I hope I need not say that if she does resolve to publish anything, I will do all in my power to relieve her from all trouble which can possibly be spared her. But to *persuade* her to publish anything I cannot, because this is contrary to my views and to my convictions.

Nevertheless, in 1836, out of six piano pieces she had composed, Fanny sent two of her favorites to London to Felix's friend, Karl Klingemann, while Felix was away on tour. Felix and Karl shared living quarters whenever Felix visited London. Feeling less restrained than if she were writing to her brother, Fanny admitted to Klingemann that in Berlin, "maybe once a year someone will copy a piece of mine, or ask me to play something special."

Now that Rebecka has left off singing, my songs lie unheeded and unknown. Without some response, in time not only all pleasure of them, but all power of judging their value is lost. Felix who is alone a sufficient public for me, is so seldom here that he cannot help me much, and thus I am thrown back entirely on myself.

Only her delight in music and her husband's sympathy had kept her working, she told Karl. "It must be a sign of talent that I do not give it up."

The reason for Fanny's self-doubts are easy to understand, but why did Felix have such a wavering attitude toward his talented sister? Was it his belief that he was sparing Fanny the harsh criticism he and other composers were sometimes subjected to? Was it his belief that Fanny would be more unhappy if she complicated her domestic life with a profession? Or was there also a sense of guilt at succeeding when his talented sister could not? Perhaps he was still clinging to his father's perception of women's place in their society. Apparently he gave no thought to the idea that more recognition would enrich her life, as it had his. Time and time again he assured himself that his view of Fanny was right. As he once expressed it:

> Fanny has neither inclination nor vocation for authorship. She is too much all that a woman ought to be for this. She regulates her house, and neither thinks of the public nor of the musical world, nor even of music at all, until her first duties are fulfilled. Publishing would only disturb her in these, and I cannot say that I approve of it.

Although the battle within grew more desperate as she grew older, Fanny's deep affection for her brother barely diminished. Now, more than before, it was up to Fanny to find time to visit him in Leipzig. But Fanny's obligations at home increased when Rebecka, who suffered bouts of depression, moved in with the Hensels after the death of her husband, bringing along her mother-in-law and four small children. Fanny sometimes begged Felix to steal away for a day to give her a day-long account of "all your activities and share the wonderful things you've experienced. Either come here for a few days *incognito* and tell us absolutely everything over an entire day, or if that's not possible [send] a long, detailed letter. In short, let us share the many wonderful things you've experienced." Then, like the young sixteen-year-old who had wanted to be told everything about Felix's first trip, she said "give me an idea of how two thousand men's voices sound—I know very well how ten sound." Felix had been conducting an oratorio in Cologne using this incredibly large choir. His answer came by letter, of course, saying "as far as that goes it was no louder than any choir, but . . . there was a certain whirr and rush, just as thirty violins are no louder than *ten*, but more penetrating and more massive."

"I am quite busy with my music and am enjoying it immensely," Fanny wrote later that same year. "I had thought that such pleasure was only a thing of the past and am truly very happy with my life."

So Fanny herself seemed to waver about her need for public recognition but she never doubted that without music her life would be bleak. As with Clara Schumann, music was not a luxury, it was a necessity.

The question of publishing came up again almost ten years later when Fanny turned forty-one. Until then she had agreed only twice to requests to publish some of her compositions, one song in a collection of works, and a year later eleven pieces consisting of songs, a piano trio, and other piano works. Then nothing more for the next nine years.

In her most touching and poignant letter Fanny begged again for understanding from Felix. In July of 1846 she wrote:

> I have to tell you something. But since I know from the start you won't like it, it's a bit awkward to get underway. So laugh at me or not, as you wish: I'm as afraid of my brother at age forty as I was of Father at age fourteen—or more precisely, eager to please you. . . . and when I already know that this will not be so, I feel rather uncomfortable. In a word, I'm beginning to publish. I have given my approval to Herr Bock's kind offer to publish my songs. I hope I won't disgrace all of you . . . I hope you won't think badly of me.

Fanny's plaintive request for understanding from Felix, and her attempt to reassure him that he needn't take any responsibility for her actions, were her final effort to win her brother's blessings. If she succeeded and received other offers to publish, she told him, it would be a great stimulus to her creativity. He, of all the family, must surely have understood this. In fact, not long after Fanny's compositions were published, she wrote in her diary, "At last Felix has written, and given me his professional blessings. . . . I know that he is not quite satisfied in his heart of hearts, but I am glad he has said a kind word to me about it."

After so many years of dismissive negative answers, her brother's reply, sent in August of 1846, sounded like the Felix she loved and remembered. Calling her "my dearest *Fance*," he sent his blessings on becoming a professional composer.

> Not until today, just as I am on the point of starting, do I, unnatural brother that I am, find time to thank you for your charming letter, and send you my professional blessings on becoming a member of the craft. This I do now in full, Fance, and may you have much happiness in giving pleasure to others; may you taste only the sweets and none of the bitterness of authorship. May the public pelt you with roses and never with sand; and may the printer's ink never draw black lines on your soul—all of which I devoutly believe will be the case, so what is the use of my wishing it! But it is the custom of the guild, so take my blessing under my hand and seal.

He then signed his letter as *journeyman tailor*, Felix Mendelssohn-Bartholdy, probably a private joke between them. He ended with a postscript suggesting music that

Fanny might interpret with "your expressive hands" at her Sunday concert in the upcoming year. In the letter, dated August 1846, he promised a visit in the autumn. Sadly, this stimulus came too late, for Fanny's time had nearly run out. Even today most of her music has never been published and remains hidden away in libraries or private collections.

∞ *Chapter 9* ∞

Spring 1847

God help us all—since yesterday I don't know what else to say and think.

Felix Mendelssohn, May 19, 1847

Felix, thoroughly exhausted after his journey to England to conduct his new oratorio *Elijah*, was forced to take a much needed rest when he returned to Leipzig. This time his wife and doctor were not persuaded by Felix's promise that when he turned forty, almost three years away, he'd spend more time with his family and less time working and traveling.

In contrast to her brother's frantic pace, Fanny's life during the spring and summer of 1846 had been remarkably pleasant. A warmer than usual spring brought with it an abundance of flowers and Fanny spent more of her free time in the garden. "[I feel] like a child again . . . happiness which is always eluding our grasp." Hinting in a letter to Cecile, Felix's wife, that a winter in their house is no joy with its drafty glass windows and doors, she said they had a right to "some compensation." This sudden, new happiness she compared with the joy she felt in Rome, the last time she had left her house and garden for more than a few days. "I begin to fear that I am too placid, and am getting selfish, because other people's troubles no longer seem to interfere with my comfort."

Fanny,
from a sketch by
Wilhelm Hensel

Fanny placid, unconcerned? Perhaps, but not idle for she was never able to remain so for long. Her upbringing left too strong a mark on her for that. She had worked a great deal that winter on a large-scale work for piano, violin, and violoncello, which was performed in April in honor of Rebecka's birthday. This score was carefully stacked in her music room along with the music scores of her brother and friends. Inside the many folios were her own four hundred or more handwritten compositions.

Adjoining the music room was her husband's studio where she could hear him at work, methodically adding paint to his large canvases.

The following winter of 1847 was harsh, full of frost and snow—and suffering. Affairs in German politics were again disturbing. The general discontent of intellectuals and German and Austrian peasants, who still made up the over-whelming mass of the population, increased the pressure on their rulers for change. Though no longer called serfs and now free, peasants were no better off than before. Since they were unable to own land, they were forced to pay high rent to their wealthy landlords. When the harvest was poor, they were left with almost nothing. In 1847, for the second year in a row, this was just what occurred and near starvation trig-gered massive discontent and anger against the rulers. The time seemed ripe for revolution. In the winter of 1848 Parisian workers would take to the streets, with protests spreading to Germany a few months later. Fanny could see the danger political change could have for her family, but tried to dismiss it because she had achieved a kind of con-tentment within her own private world.

What have we done to deserve being among the few happy ones in the world? My inmost heart is full of thankfulness, and when, in the morning after breakfast with Wilhelm, we each go to our own work, with a pleasant day to look back upon, and another to look forward to, I am quite overcome with my own happiness.

On a Friday afternoon in May 1847, while rehearsing a small choir for the next Sunday's music program, Fanny suddenly fell ill. Her hands dropped from the piano to her sides, and she was unable to talk. Shortly afterward, she lost consciousness and she died that evening. The suddenness with which she went was a terrible shock to her family. Felix, leaving England tired and exhausted saying "another week like this, and I'm a dead man," returned to the continent to find a letter telling him of Fanny's death. With a cry he collapsed to the floor.

For Fanny's husband it was an irreparable loss. Their days had been spent working almost side by side from the beginning of their marriage. They had a loving, trusting relationship based on admiration for each other's talent. In addition, Fanny had taken care of all of Hensel's business matters, the management of the house and property, and family problems. Though Hensel had enough commissions for paintings to keep him busy for the next several years, he lost all interest in his work and never even completed the large painting that was nearly finished. His son wrote that he never painted anything worthwhile during the fifteen years that he survived Fanny.

Felix, stunned by her death and feeling at last a sense of guilt, arranged to have more of Fanny's music published. "There is no doubt," wrote Felix, "[the publisher] would consider it an honor to be able to see such works published by his firm . . . please tell Hensel all of this."

But this gesture of remorse after years of refusing his consent and blessings was too insignificant to have much effect on the future appreciation of his sister's music. What she had been seeking from him for so long, his support for having her music published and recognized, came too late.

> My dearest Rebecka [wrote Felix the day after hearing about Fanny's death], how often since yesterday I have regretted not having been in Berlin with all of you more often . . . for I have also lost my best friend. I know well that she loved me, that I could count on her as on solid rock, and that she would never have deserted me. But she is no longer among the living, and I shall never again see her beautiful eyes. God help us all.

Felix never recovered his health and died only six months after Fanny, just as suddenly, from a stroke on November 4, 1847. He was only thirty-eight. He was buried by her side in a churchyard in Berlin. At the funeral Rebecka and Paul were stricken when they recalled that Felix had promised Fanny the year before that he would be with her on her birthday, November fourteen. "Count on it, the next time I'll be with you."

Many of Felix Mendelssohn's last works were published after his death. His music continues to be heard and performed regularly to this day.

Fanny's music has just begun to be rediscovered.

Epilogue

*H*ow much has the music world changed for women since the time of Fanny Mendelssohn? How many more opportunities are there today for women to compose, conduct, or to have their music performed?

Although women musicians have taken their place among men on the concert stage as members of symphony orchestras, in chamber music groups, and as soloists, it is still relatively rare for women to conduct orchestras or have their music performed in concerts. But women have taken up the challenge to break down the old barriers. Today the number of women composers, performers, teachers, and arts managers has increased considerably, though it is still far behind that of their male counterparts. Here are the stories of some of the women who have defied tradition, and have earned the respect of the music world as musical pioneers.

*I*n Italy in 1857, ten years after Fanny's death, a twenty-year-old Italian woman named Carlotta Ferrari composed an opera called *Ugo*. When she realized that no company would perform her opera, Ms. Ferrari paid for the entire production on her own in order to see it performed. At its premier, *Ugo* was a huge success, but she was never able to recover the enormous expense of the production, nor did she hear it performed again. She died at age seventy in 1907.

Cécile Chaminade, born in Paris in 1861, unlike Carlotta Ferrari, lived a long and productive life. Most of her music was published during her lifetime and received much popular attention. She toured Europe performing many of her own compositions, but they were only a small fraction of her 350 works, which included ballet music, an opera, and a choral symphony. Chaminade died in Monte Carlo in 1944 at the age of eighty-three.

In the United States, Amy Beach, born in Henniker, New Hampshire, in 1867, was, for the late nineteenth and early twentieth centuries, a remarkably successful composer. Her first public appearance as a pianist was with the Boston Symphony Orchestra at age sixteen. With only modest training in music theory she began composing large works: a symphony, a mass, and concertos that were performed widely by major orchestras in the United States. The story goes that she taught herself counterpoint and fugue by writing out from memory much of Bach's Well-Tempered Clavier, then comparing her version to Bach's. Some of her classical piano training came from a teacher who had been a student of Ignaz Mosheles, Felix's and Fanny's old friend.

Beach continued to compose into her seventies. By her example she encouraged and actively supported many women composers of her day. She died in 1944.

Wanda Landowska, born in 1879 in Warsaw, Poland, was an outstanding performer on the harpsichord and piano. The first modern works for harpsichord were written for her by the Spanish composer Manuel de Falla and by Francis Poulenc of France. She has been credited with restoring interest in the harpsichord through her many performances on the concert stage. The last years of her life were spent in the United States. She died in 1959.

In France, the Boulanger sisters, Nadia, born in 1887, and Lili, born in 1893, came from a musical family. Their father taught voice in the Paris Conservatory and Raissa, their mother, was a singer. Nadia, who both composed and taught music, was the first woman to conduct the Boston Symphony Orchestra in 1937 and the New York Philharmonic in 1939. In 1950, she was appointed director of the American Conservatory in Fountainbleau, France, and became world renowned as the teacher of some of the foremost composers and performers of the twentieth century. Nadia Boulanger lived to the age of ninety-two.

Lili Boulanger won the Prix de Rome, open to all young composers, for her cantata *Faust et Helene* in 1913, at age nineteen. Five years later another of her compositions won the prize only to be taken away because the contest was then open to unmarried *men only*. She had sent her unsigned music in defiance of the contest rules because she felt them unfair. She died at age twenty-five, leaving over fifty works, including piano, orchestral, choral works, and an opera.

Margaret Sutherland, born in 1897, repeated the route Fanny Hensel had taken to have her work heard by performing her own compositions at private concerts. In 1925, she said, no one wanted to hear new music in Australia. She survived for over forty years with almost no encouragement by teaching music and giving informal concerts. She died in 1984, having composed an opera called *The Young Kabbarli*, and choral, piano, orchestral, and chamber works.

Ruth Crawford Seeger, born in 1901 in Ohio, was the first woman composer to win a Guggenheim Fellowship. She transcribed six thousand American folksongs from field recordings for which she composed over three hundred piano accompaniments. The collection is now at the Library of Congress. Besides her more ambitious instrumental works she wrote folksongs especially for children. Ms. Seeger died in 1953.

Julia Smith, a native of Texas, born a few years before World War I in 1911, was one of seven children. She, like Fanny and Felix, received her first lessons from her mother. After getting her master's degree from the Juilliard School of Music in New York City, she applied to the school for a fellowship to study composition.

"I have decided not to waste any more of Juilliard's money on fellowships for women," said her prospective teacher. "All you gifted women composers come to New York, study a few years, then go back home, get married, have children, and that is the last one ever hears of them as composers."

Julia Smith's answer was *but not this one!* After finishing her studies, she then went on to compose a large number of works to prove him wrong.

Sarah Caldwell, born in Maryville, Missouri, in 1924, began to study the violin at age four. By age five, she was performing with adult groups. She conducted her first opera as an assistant at the New England Opera Company and was later appointed director of the Boston University Opera, introducing new operas by American and European composers to her audiences. Caldwell has been a guest conductor of numerous symphony orchestras from New York City to Beijing.

*　*　*

In the United States the first efforts of Emma Lou Diemer to compose music were at age seven. By the age of thirteen, she was composing full-scale piano concertos. She wrote:

> There was no time in my life that I didn't love music and playing the piano. During high school I would write music in the morning before going to classes, because the house was quiet and I was alone. . . . Every Sunday afternoon I would listen to the broadcast of the New York Philharmonic Orchestra and reflect on the compositions I heard. When I decided to become a composer, I knew there were great men composers and naturally I would become a woman composer.

Professor Diemer composed about one hundred forty works including symphonies, choral music, concertos, quartets, and songs. She is also a distinguished performer on the organ, harpsichord, and piano.

Israeli musician Dalia Atlas, born in 1935, said she knew she wanted to be a conductor but her teachers discouraged her from pursuing this career. They said it was hard work for a man, "and for a woman there would be no justice; I would not be allowed to conduct." But Dalia Atlas persisted and later won *five* conducting competitions in Europe.

Composer Joan Tower, born in New Rochelle, New York, in 1938, has been called one of the most successful composers of her generation. Her most popular symphonic compositions are *Sequoia*, composed in 1981, and *Silver Ladders*. *Fanfare for the Uncommon Woman* was written in 1986 for the Houston Symphony and has been performed over one hundred times.

Tower was composer-in-residence at the St. Louis

Symphony from 1985 to 1987 and is currently a professor of music at Bard College in New York State.

Ellen Taaffe Zwilich, born in 1939, said, "There was a piano in my home that I discovered before I learned to walk." During her childhood she spent much of her time improvising and making up pieces on the piano.

After graduating with a master's degree in composition from Florida State University, she went to New York to study violin and later became a member of the American Symphony Orchestra under the well-known conductor Leopold Stokowski.

In 1975, the Juilliard School of Music conferred its first doctorate degree in composition for a woman on thirty-six-year-old Ellen Zwilich, ending the exclusiveness of male recipients of this degree.

In the book *Women Composers, Conductors, and Musicians of the Twentieth Century*, the author Jane Weiner Lepage gives a list of the compositions written by each of the fifty-two women artists mentioned. The list, by now, is surely incomplete. Many music lovers are still unaware of this music because it has had too little exposure. As opportunities grow, we will hear more works by contemporary women composers as well as rediscovered works of such artists as Fanny Mendelssohn Hensel.

Musical Terms

Clavier: A musical instrument with a keyboard, such as a harpsichord, piano, or organ.

Fugue: A musical composition that uses a single melodic idea introduced several times in a multivoiced manner. The best-known fugues were written by Bach and Handel.

Lieder: German songs of the nineteenth century based on poems or stories. The style is romantic.

Opera: A play that is sung along with orchestral accompaniment. Opera first began in Italy at the end of the 1500s.

Oratorio: Music based mostly on religious themes using solo singers, a chorus, and an orchestra performing together or in turn, first performed in the *Oratory* of St. Philip Neri, Rome, in the early seventeenth century.

Overture: Usually a short instrumental piece used as an introduction to an opera, ballet, or any larger musical work. The word comes from the French word *ouverture,* meaning "opening."

Sonata: From the Italian word *suonare* "to sound." A composition for a solo keyboard instrument, or keyboard and one other solo instrument. If it includes more than two instruments, three for example, it will be called a trio, for four, a quartet.

Symphony: A large orchestral work usually but not always composed of three or more parts or *movements.*

Selected Bibliography

Blunt, Wilfred. *On Wings of Song.* New York: Scribner Sons, 1974.

Citron, Marcia, translator. *The Letters of Fanny Hensel to Felix Mendelssohn.* Stuyvesant, N.Y.: Pendragon Press, 1987.

Cohen, Aaron I. *International Encyclopedia of Women Composers.* New York: Books & Music, Inc., 1987.

Crocker, Annette E., translator. *An Autobiography—Charles Gounod.* Chicago, New York: Rand McNally & Co., 1895.

Elvers, Rudolph. *Felix Mendelssohn, A Life in Letters.* New York: Fromm International Publishing Co., 1986.

Erskine, John. *Songs Without Words.* New York: Julian Messner, 1941.

Hensel, Sebastian. *Die Familie Mendelssohn*, Vol. I, II. New York: Harper & Bros., 1882, 1895.

Hurd, Michael. *Mendelssohn.* New York: Thomas Y. Crowell Co., 1970.

Jezic, Diane Peacock. *Women Composers, The Lost Tradition Found.* New York: The Feminist Press, 1988.

Kupferberg, Herbert. *Felix Mendelssohn, His Life, His Family, His Music.* New York: Scribner Sons, 1972.

Lampadius, Wilhelm. *The Life of Felix Mendelssohn.* New York and Philadelphia: Frederick Leypoldt, 1865.

Lepage, Jane Weiner. *Women Composers, Conductors, and Musicians of the Twentieth Century.* Metuchen, N.J.: Scarecrow Press, 1980.

Neuls-Bates, Carol. *Women in Music.* New York: Harper & Row, 1982.

Reich, Nancy B. *Clara Schumann, The Artist and the Woman.* Ithaca, N.Y.: Cornell University Press, 1985.

Todd, R. Larry, editor. *Mendelssohn and His World.* Princeton, N.J.: Princeton University Press, 1991.

Werner, Eric. *Mendelssohn.* London: The Free Press of Glencoe, Collier/Macmillan, 1963.

Index